This book belongs to

English - Vietnamese

duck   Date _____

con vịt

duck

duck
duck
duck
duck
duck

con vịt

Make a sentence

horse　　　　　　Date _____

con ngựa　　　

horse   con ngựa
_____   _____
horse ....
_____   _____
horse ....
_____   _____
horse ....
_____   _____
horse ....
_____   _____
horse ....
_____   _____

Make a sentence

_____
....
_____
....
_____
....
_____
....
_____
....
_____
....
_____

mouse Date _____

chuột

mouse

chuột

mouse

mouse

mouse

mouse

mouse

Make a sentence

wolf

Date _____

chó sói

wolf

chó sói

wolf

wolf

wolf

wolf

wolf

Make a sentence

panda   Date _____

gấu trúc

panda

gấu trúc

panda

panda

panda

panda

panda

Make a sentence

chicken

gà

chicken

gà

chicken

chicken

chicken

chicken

chicken

Make a sentence

dinosaur

Date _____

khủng long

dinosaur

dinosaur
dinosaur
dinosaur
dinosaur
dinosaur

khủng long

Make a sentence

elephant

Date _____

con voi

elephant

elephant
elephant
elephant
elephant
elephant

con voi

Make a sentence

cow

Date _____

bò

cow

cow

cow

cow

cow

cow

bò

Make a sentence

butterfly

Con bướm

butterfly

Con bướm

butterfly

butterfly

butterfly

butterfly

butterfly

Make a sentence

worm

Date _____

sâu

worm

sâu

worm

worm

worm

worm

worm

Make a sentence

puppy   Date_____

cún yêu

puppy

cún yêu

puppy

puppy

puppy

puppy

puppy

Make a sentence

turtle   Date _____

rùa

turtle

rùa

turtle

turtle

turtle

turtle

turtle

Make a sentence

turkey

Date _____

gà tây

turkey   gà tây

turkey

turkey

turkey

turkey

turkey

Make a sentence

hippopotamus

Date_____

Hà mã

hippopotamus Hà mã

hippopotamus

hippopotamus

hippopotamus

hippopotamus

hippopotamus

Make a sentence

tiger

Date _____

con hổ

tiger

con hổ

tiger

tiger

tiger

tiger

tiger

Make a sentence

hen   Date_____

gà mái

hen

gà mái

hen
hen
hen
hen
hen

Make a sentence

alligator

Date _____

cá sấu

alligator

cá sấu

alligator

alligator

alligator

alligator

alligator

Make a sentence

monkey

con khỉ

monkey

monkey

monkey

monkey

monkey

monkey

con khỉ

Make a sentence

spider   Date _____

nhện

spider

nhện

spider

spider

spider

spider

spider

Make a sentence

shark   Date _____

cá mập

shark

cá mập

shark

shark

shark

shark

shark

Make a sentence

lion

Date_____

sư tử

lion

sư tử

lion

lion

lion

lion

lion

Make a sentence

snail

Date _____

ốc

snail

óc

snail

snail

snail

snail

snail

Make a sentence

kangaroo

Date _____

Kangaroo

kangaroo   Kangaroo

kangaroo

kangaroo

kangaroo

kangaroo

kangaroo

Make a sentence

fox

Date _____

cáo

fox

cáo

fox

fox

fox

fox

fox

Make a sentence

snake   Date _____

con rắn

snake   con rắn

snake

snake

snake

snake

snake

Make a sentence

camel

Date _____

lạc đà

camel   lạc đà

camel

camel

camel

camel

camel

Make a sentence

octopus

Date _____

bạch tuộc

octopus

bạch tuộc

octopus

octopus

octopus

octopus

octopus

Make a sentence

rooster

Date _____

gà trống

rooster

gà trống

rooster

rooster

rooster

rooster

rooster

Make a sentence

kitten   Date _____

mèo con

kitten

kitten
kitten
kitten
kitten
kitten

mèo con

Make a sentence

deer   Date _____

con nai

deer

con nai

deer

deer

deer

deer

deer

Make a sentence

ant

kiến

ant   kiến

ant

ant

ant

ant

ant

Make a sentence

dog Date _____

chó

dog

chó

dog

dog

dog

dog

dog

Make a sentence

giraffe   Date_____

hươu cao cổ

giraffe   hươu cao cổ

giraffe

giraffe

giraffe

giraffe

giraffe

Make a sentence

cat

con mèo

cat

con mèo

cat

cat

cat

cat

cat

Make a sentence

crab

Date _____

cua

crab

cua

crab

crab

crab

crab

crab

Make a sentence

zebra   Date _____

ngựa rằn

zebra

ngựa rằn

zebra

zebra

zebra

zebra

zebra

Make a sentence

eagle Date_____

chim ưng

eagle

chim ưng

eagle

eagle

eagle

eagle

eagle

Make a sentence

rabbit

Date _____

Con thỏ

rabbit

Con thỏ

rabbit

rabbit

rabbit

rabbit

rabbit

Make a sentence

sheep   Date _____

cừu

sheep

cừu

sheep

sheep

sheep

sheep

sheep

Make a sentence

fish

cá

fish

cá

fish

fish

fish

fish

fish

Make a sentence

bird   Date _____

chim

bird

bird

bird

bird

bird

bird

chim

Make a sentence

dolphin   Date_____

cá heo

dolphin

cá heo

dolphin

dolphin

dolphin

dolphin

dolphin

Make a sentence

bee   Date _____

con ong

bee

con ong

bee

bee

bee

bee

Make a sentence

hedgehog

Date _____

nhím

hedgehog   nhím

hedgehog

hedgehog

hedgehog

hedgehog

hedgehog

Make a sentence

lobster

Date_____

tôm hùm

lobster   tôm hùm

lobster

lobster

lobster

lobster

lobster

Make a sentence

owl

Date_____

cú

owl

cú

owl

owl

owl

owl

owl

Make a sentence

frog   Date _____

ếch

frog   éch

frog

frog

frog

frog

frog

Make a sentence

pig

Date_____

con lợn

pig

con lợn

pig

pig

pig

pig

pig

Make a sentence

goat

Date _____

con dê

goat

goat

goat

goat

goat

goat

goat

con dê

Make a sentence

dragonfly

Date _____

con chuồn chuồn

dragonfly

con chuồn chuồn

dragonfly

dragonfly

dragonfly

dragonfly

dragonfly

Make a sentence

squirrel   Date _____

sóc

squirrel

sóc

squirrel

squirrel

squirrel

squirrel

squirrel

Make a sentence

parrot   Date _____

con vẹt

parrot

con vẹt

parrot

parrot

parrot

parrot

parrot

Make a sentence

Made in United States
North Haven, CT
03 August 2023